AF247573

From the Diary of Peter Doyle

and other poems

John Gill

ALEMBIC PRESS · PLAINFIELD, INDIANA

Other books by John Gill:

Young Man's Letter (1967, New/Books, The Crossing Press)
Gill's Blues (1969, New/Books, The Crossing Press)
Country Pleasures (1975, The Crossing Press)

Edited:

New American and Canadian Poetry (1971, Beacon Press)

The author thanks the following periodicals for first publishing some of the poems included in this book: *Alembic, Common Sense, Hanging Loose, Mickle Street Review, Poetry Now, Roberson Poetry Annual.*

Author and publisher thank the Walt Whitman Association for providing the photograph of Walt Whitman and Peter Doyle which is reproduced on the cover and frontispiece.

Publication of this book was made possible in part by a grant from the National Endowment for the Arts, a Federal agency.

Design and typography: David Dayton
Printed in the U.S.A. by McNaughton & Gunn

Library of Congress CIP Data

Gill, John, 1924–
    From the diary of Peter Doyle and other poems.

    I. Title.
PS3557.I369F7   811'.52   81-12770
ISBN 0-934184-13-5 (hardcover)   AACR2
ISBN 0-934184-14-3 (paperback)

1   2   3   4   5

Contents

1

A Gloss on Four Lines from Chilam-Balam

it will be the time when he
takes the road . . .

your thumbs are heavy
and your eye-sockets have caved in
your hair is thin and brittle
your eyes can't judge properly any more
everything is too small or too large or clouded
your feet tingle when you lie down
your balls have dried up   your stomach
floats like a fetid swamp
full of hungry crocodiles
yet your appetite longs for the desert
where it envies the cactus its dry ether
your nose has lost its taste for air
and your tongue is so tired it sinks
to the bottom of your mouth in a hiss

is it the time to give up direction
to take the road as if it were a cloud
that would lead you to the city
of mythic towers where angels with eyes
like birds of prey and the vanity of peacocks
patrol the streets and speak with forked lightning

or is it the time to shrink into a ball and roll
back to fetal perfection: tiny nails, tiny toes,
spongy rubber face squinting against the light
saying, no, no, no   I will or I will not

perhaps there is no choice as the snow comes down
in huge flakes to blot out the hereafter
but to take the road, let it find you
within the space that is left as you go.

it will be the time when he
takes the road, when he uncovers
his face . . .

at first there is nothing between your fingers
your palms held up and over . . .
not even a round O to tell you
what is missing   there might be birds
flying but can they fly and not move,
frozen   in this condition you are erased
the stutter of a universe away
and no spark yet made
that can draw a line, drive a wedge,
reveal — so you despair utterly
uncover an inward abyss so cavernous and deep
that you hover at its edge, afraid

but like a child you are now conscious
of space, the stupified attention
it brings, your fingers opening like slats
your eyes like black moons rising
the sharp ridge and sieve of your nose touching air
your ears poking through like question marks
your cheeks hung like apples on a bough
your lips a blessed wound about to bleed
but this is before talk, before your chin advances
before your whole face becomes light.

it will be the time when he
takes the road, when he uncovers
his face and talks and vomits
what he swallowed . . .

talk bubbles endlessly
it tickles the throat like a swallowed hair
like a gate it swings loosely in the breeze
it spills over in arabesques and filigrees
of lace, it dances in parody, it stomps
on your feeling with sharp nails, it
bleeds like an ulcer, "baas" like a lamb,
shuts like a door, insidious as a thin moon
deceptive as a surface—try gliding on it—
it is what you do when you open your mouth
and mice pop out to run around the room
shitting in corners—a nasty business

it can also soothe by its own music
can write whole scales of love and pain
it is often lonely as a dove in the pines
as witnessing as the stars and as loud
so when you begin to talk, beware,
the flood is loosened and steaming
clots, phrases, sentences, structures
are vomited on the world everything
you swallowed alive must cross the wire
back again making a possible life.

it will be the time when he
takes the road, when he uncovers
his face and talks and vomits
what he swallowed and lays down his load

back from the dead and you lay
down your load in humble pain
your unwitting gift, certainly unwanted,
that you earned   whatever dodge you invented
whatever dream that stuck like honey
to your pores that would not break down
whatever fact you rubbed against till
it shone like a mirror reflecting your face
and that you followed at a distance
like a faithful dog its master

you are cindered and burnt, the classic journey
completed: over chasms, across underground rivers
to fight with the beast, you are ripped to pieces
to still stand upright
confirmed in folly and cursing life
embracing the dark lord but spat out
you return to the light   the road ahead
has more to acknowledge than you can
see, your eyelids like butterflies
your hands tentative but groping it is time
to take the road, unwind it from your
self and go wherever it leads
to lay down your load in humble pain.

An Old Story

Adam watched the animals coupling, the ox ponderous and awkward climbing its mate to become a two-backed creature frozen against the sky. He watched the birds flutter up and mate in air. He watched a turtle dig a trench and fill it to the top with eggs. He watched a lion cuff its mate and snarl to be obeyed. He saw flowers open and scatter yellow gold. Then watched the bees rummage the blooms drunkenly. But nothing stirred in him. Or if he smiled it was unconsciously, feeling the nights he lay with Eve as warmth and satisfaction, nothing more.

Eve was light as a shadow that runs ahead or lags behind dependent on which way Adam shone. Her life was easy, filled with the singing that comes from unquestioned devotion.

Yet Adam was bored and Eve was bored by the lowing, cooing, munching of animals, the bright, genial sun, the waxy, perfect flowers, the lush climbing plants, the diamond-studded grass in early light, the pure, penetrable sky, the dimpled streams and gaping fish. They wanted something undefinably more by the end of what seemed forever, for – though time had no meaning here, everything went on serenely, endlessly – both Adam and Eve would frown when they remembered God's injunction not to eat the fruit of the tree of the knowledge of good and evil.

The apple is almost perfect. Its umbilical and flower ends dip into navels that swell with fruit. One night Eve was startled from sleep when an apple fell with a soft thud into the lap of the earth. Her heart caught; then fell in the same trajectory. She suddenly remembered stars on cloudless nights – her gasp of delight when one would arc in the sky and go out. But the apple was different – it wasn't faraway light! It fell with an abrupt thud that entered her. She listened a long time that night for the next apple to drop from the tree. She wanted to feel it again: the silence, the falling, the final reach, so strange – like her breasts, like her own body, open under the sky.

Notes on the Divided Life

what to make of you?
what to make of the line of descent
that splits you from head to toe?
the sinister left, the perfect right
those askew mirror images.
you catch each other looking:
which is the model? which the stranger?
there must be something wrong, wasn't I made whole?
no, you answer, you are bi-polar
starting with the soft spot on the top of your head.
you should realize your omnipresent danger
for though that bubbling crater closed
in infancy, it's there the egg
splits and flows. like gouging fruit
your two thumbs can crack it along lines
that spread and lay it open.
here the line of division runs:
the twin eyeballs, cleft nose,
hairy tubes of air exposed, cleft chin,
ears trying to stabilize, flapping at the verge,
the matching shoulders, the arms,
rib-cages, the lungs in sacs — they store
the moon and the sun. next, the miracle:
the belly-button, the Buddha hall of delights
that threatens to fuse the world again
but the double hips, the smooth thighs betray,
the rapid line of descent, the cock, the weighty balls
dangle at the edge where the long split yawns
and vertigo! down the legs to grasp the earth
separately, the feet with splayed toes pointing.
the gingerbread man rolled out, that's you,
frightened, still surviving upright
leading your double, your divided life.
your subtle buttocks following you everywhere.

A Short Prayer

if not with the jerky lightness of a butterfly
or the suavity of an angel
then, at least, lord of my destiny,
let me rise with some animal energy and cunning
not lie here sullen, convinced
it's better not to rise at all
while I grind my teeth and belong
neither to the forgiving breast of the earth
nor to the free grace of the air.

Notes for a Dawn

my back to the window I feel dawn rising
like a cosmic egg about to be laid.
terrifying, not at all picturesque.
a dim fuse of light starts the process.
no matter how I turn in bed there's
no escaping. if challenged it is
a presence that is not. here
and yet not here. on a level
below silence. a boil. a fungus
of light whose spores are spreading.
I feel it now on my face as dots.
a giant hum behind it.
galactic machinery moving.
oh. please bring release. please.
there is so much saturated that
waits to be born.

Las Vegas Jolted By Nuclear Test

Mercury, Nevada (AP) — An underground nuclear test at the Nevada Test Site produced a rolling earth tremor that shook Las Vegas, 120 miles to the south, for about 30 seconds this morning.

The nuclear device, with at least ten times the force of the bomb that destroyed Hiroshima during World War II, was exploded 2,800 feet beneath the desert in the Pahute Mesa area of the test site.

There were no problems reported from the test.

1. *The Old Man*

an old man reading in a big house.
his dog groans and twitches in her sleep.
his mother had died in her sleep.
she hated death and funerals—left notes.
no eulogies. no ceremonies. please
no music or mourning friends.
his stomach fell—earth tremors through
the pit when he read.
where was the shame?
the shaking apart of the frame? could
he walk out the door and not feel
the earth convulsing as his feet stepped down
from the threshold to the ground?
he had died in his sleep and was walking a
dream. it was almost spring.
birds sifting through the hedge.
mist rising from the pit where
she lay aborting. rocks? teeth?
liquid guts? oh   mother. mother.
flinching even in his dream.
the pond across the road sent
glinting needles that sewed up his eyes.
he had expected tears
some heave of weight that
would swallow or expunge. an
alimentary death. messy. slimy. gasping.
but no. the earth tremors were
a dream sadness with him always.
a black, scavenger bird
flitted away from a tree. spring
almost here and the signs where were
the signs? did his feet touch the ground?

2. *One of Those Involved*

first a small hole is bored
into the earth
and fine grit spumes up
in a steady flow.
little grit hills accumulate.

it is smooth even work
barring sudden jolts when
the bit hits rock
then it's hang hard and jarring chug.

the grit fountain flows.
the little grit hills accumulate

until it's 2,800 feet deep
a thin breathing-hole
leading into darkness.

we cap our ear to it
hear the vacuum roar
of what it promises.

our probe is almost ready.
we lower our charge.
we lower our instruments.
we fill her up
and tamp her down.

then we hide and push the button
—the big blow
the rumbling black freight's
muffled KA-BOOM

rolling tremors south
to jolt the gamblers in Vegas.
there are no problems.
we've hit the jack-pot!

3. *The Site*

Pahute Mesa does not support life.
it's dead land the government claims
chain-linked and barb-wired
for experimental purposes.
the reality of its death
who can name it?
the social bees that taste the desert flower?
the hawks buzzards rabbits
rattlers rodents that live there?
sand rock cactus old Indian bones?
the dry-furnace heat that's so alive?
this meeting-place of mesa and sky
like a grand tableau?
or is it the government? did they kill it?
chain-link and barb-wire
it out of existence. dead.
so we drive around. no messages go.
no messages arrive.
not even Mercury could lead us
from this world to that
without tight security badges
and once we got there what would
we say to the busy dead
making their arrangements
monitoring their instruments?
"Pahute Mesa lives," we would say,
"forget this obscene probe.
look, for the sake of the gods, look
around you. the earth is alive."
as if we were speaking to children
who were listening. but
we are talking to technicians.
their eyes swim in data.
this is not the land of the sacred dead
but land the never-born claim
for experimental purposes.

4. *The earth and myself are of one mind.*
                              —Chief Joseph

the dead have spoken their mind.
as a herd galloping over the edge
thunder in their words but their
voices thin. we barely hear them.
that is the lure
voices of the dead calling us
to life.
Chief Joseph's arrogance.
the look in his eyes
shines back at us
from the bottom of the hole.
the sun on our backs
we squat looking down
at the light. somehow
it's under our feet. transformed.

5. *The Old Man Again*

a spring day more certain than the others
worms rising to be fed   birds
busy in the garden. there was a knock
at the door. a young woman in grey
carrying a satchel. she said, "I'd like
to share some words with you." taking
out her black book pointing to Luke
ch. 21, verse 25:

And there shall be signs in sun and moon and
stars; and upon the earth distress of nations,
in perplexity for the roaring of the sea and the
billows; men fainting for fear, and for
expectation of the things which are coming
on the world: for the powers of the heavens
shall be shaken.

he rocked back on his heels
saying, "I feel pretty good, pretty hopeful."
knowing it sounded insipid   wanting
to counter her gloom and her remedy
Jesus coming in a cloud to save
the witnesses. she was bent
on her truth and he didn't know.
they stood there in loose company
muddy ground and balmy sky
the last earth tremors fading away
out west. or just beginning.

11/19/79

coming off the inner loop 490 into Rochester you suddenly find yourself in narrow streets. on the right a municipal parking lot and a senior citizen's center. once a furniture store. on the left is a church facing a square with a dry fountain. you park and cross the square. three blacks lounge on a bench drinking from a paper bag. one fat one sitting down. two thin ones standing up. they are not going anywhere. that's why their casualness is so elaborate. it's close to violence and despair. that's why you cross the street to walk by the church.

such immaculate grounds and parish house. the windows shine. the dark shades drawn. the paths swept. the geraniums low along the walk leading to the door. you wonder what the priest does in the cool interior silence. feed his flock? on the church door is a small decal that reads: "THESE PREMISES GUARDED BY DONOLLEY PROTECTION AGENCY."

there's a garden adjoining the church with a six-foot iron fence around it. the gate padlocked. inside are stone benches lining a path that leads to a blue grotto where on the upper rim it says in gold letters: "ST. MARY OF THE HIGHWAYS." and there she is: pale, demure, life-size terra-cotta waiting for someone like me. or like the three blacks across the street. we surely could use her blessing except we'd be out of place inside the tight ship of the church. besides the gate is chained. the garden is all angles. paving-stones and clipped to its life. you look again and there's the gardener. that privileged man locked inside. raking a leaf. seeing him you feel sad and ironic and superior.

but suddenly above you the church tower booms. the bells are striking the hour. it's 11 o'clock. my. my. there must be hope after all. we're all in this together. but why this desolation? this hanging death in the square? this organized death in the churchyard? this is Rochester. a busy industrial city. maybe churches and squares are just passé. you shrug, whispering under your breath as you leave, "goodbye, St. Mary of the Highways. pray for us. pray for us all as we drive through Rochester headed for the suburbs and the shopping malls."

8/16/80

I know a man who saves string. he creates big balls of it and piles them in corners of his trailer. whenever he finds a piece, no matter how humble, he picks it up as if his fingers were giant pincers moving in to rescue something neglected and precious. once he has it he ties and winds it carefully onto the matrix core. on and on he goes making life more complex every day.

I envy him his vision of economy and form. it's a pretty sloppy world, after all. I suspect he'll never *do* anything with the string, though. his windings satisfy a hunger to control part of the universe — here he's got loose scraps of unrelated material literally thrown to the winds. he finds them. molds them to a shape that tantalizes and soothes: a globe. completion. nourisher of life. the breast and balls of existence. mother of us all . . .

he holds the riddle in his hands: keep peeling it and what do you get? by his reverse efforts, however, the ball grows bigger and bigger and bigger, a giddy task with no end. and to think. he starts from just a tiny, useless nothing. a piece of string. and ends up with. this!

That's Entertainment

every twenty years or so Hollywood resurrects Ann Miller.
she of the long dancing legs, black lacquered hair and plastic
smile. in my childhood I could never understand why she was
in movies. she had nothing to do with the story except to turn
to the leading lady and say "cheer up, kid" or "men are all
alike." her voice was tinny. her acting stank. how could
anyone believe her?

and she always giggled and jiggled restlessly as if she
couldn't wait for the real thing to happen. what she was paid
to do and what she did. not all this other junk. but even when
she danced she was a maniac. and I liked dancing as a teen-
ager. but Ann Miller! with her tight sequinned costumes. her
long black stockings on her long spidery legs and her black
top-hat on her long midnight hair out there tapping as hard
and determined as she could tap. 500 taps a minute. and then
faster going with the frenzy she would approach her climax
and start to twirl around and around more demonic faster and
faster her smile would freeze on her chalky face her arms
straight out would snap and her torso would spin with preci-
sion till it blurred. till my eyes and head hurt. till I felt dizzy
and queasy.

but. oh. Ann Miller! when you finally stopped and took the
big bow you were as ready as ever. your set smile. your
pneumatic breasts moving slightly with just the ghost of
exertion. still game. not at all dizzy or done in. and I guess
that's why Hollywood keeps resurrecting you decade after
decade. such good machines don't die. they never get thrown
away. and as long as they run they will always amaze.

now I read that you're putting on a new Broadway show. oh.
Ann Miller! have you no decency? in your shiny black patents
you'll be racing toward your climax on my grave.

10/1/80

I don't have much to hang on to these days. living alone in a big house. lots of empty rooms. when I get home from work silence pushes in and sits down like the guest I can't get rid of. across the table looking me right in the eye. but really evasive as hell knowing it's unwanted.

I turn on the radio. make dinner. feed the cats. sometimes I dance a little jig to entertain it. I start feeling sorry for silence sucker that I am. sometimes. especially when washing myself or combing my hair. I babble to it in various tongues. it knows all languages. of course. and can appreciate any role I take: virgin girls. senile old men. evil cossacks. simpering fools. you name it. it dotes on human nature. silence would make a great audience if it only took itself seriously. but it's fickle. it gets bored and falls asleep wherever it happens to be.

then my turn comes. I unzip it. don't know how else to explain it. and climb in. we fit fine. you might think it's too tight at first but it isn't. we move together just the slightest breadth out of sync. and this is where we shine! we dialogue. we catch each other in flight. take long. windy trips across the page — I get my notebook out to keep charts. it's quite lovely. sometimes. these visits. but they don't last very long. silence gets restless. wants its freedom. what can I do! I turn on the radio. louder. this time. wash the dishes. put out the cats. and silence settles in. more dependent than ever. now. on my poor hospitality.

Having Sons

the fish-eye of comparison will not hold.
catapulted out of the tower they sing another
flight. different birds. different music. yet.
one feather from each son drifts down to match
our plumage.

it may be the lucky feather of good looks. or
the black feather of night. the feather of making
money. or the idle feather of a fool. whatever it
is it's the wrong one and it's not enough. this
particular feather of ours.

surely. we're mocked. the very presence of our
sons is an itch we have to scratch. our voices get
tense and shrill. we grow red in the face. what
did our sons do in their harmless way to provoke
us but repeat every one of our failures. and when
they are through. the list empty. the terms
exhausted. with tender love they will plow us
under where we have plowed.

and one feather of ours will cling to them. they
will wear it the rest of their lives.

An Old Chinese Saying

*So long as men have lovely children
what have they to grieve about?*

he sits on the top step in his long underwear
and squirts a stream of tobacco juice into the
yard below. imagine a serpent flicking its
forked tongue to the utmost. or a giant frog
unrolling its tongue to snag a victim. it is
done with dispatch, too—some show but no fuss.
the sun is about to rise, or to set, on another
busy day. he has nothing to grieve about. not
even lovely children.

A Teen-Age Bar

they move with the inexplicable gliding abruptness of fish in an aquarium. stopping, backing off, or mouthing quietly in small schools that disappear before your eyes.

"it's hard on them — the mating game," my friend says from behind his slouch and his beer. and I look around: the girls' movements, their nervous delicacy. the boys swirling in the currents. I understand little. they don't drink with enjoyment. they ignore the disco, their smiles and animation wooden, minimal.

yet "trees grow and flowers bloom." there must be connection, exchange, lightning strokes and rumbles that presage wind, flood, famine, death!

understated cool is in control. each boy, each girl triggered to an edge — a wrong move could blow them away. there goes Sebastian full of arrows and pity, with Ursula, she of the sacrificing heart, in his wake.

amazing ending

"How's Your Love-Life?"

for J.P.

they turn back the covers. they climb in. everything in place.
battened down for the night. the lemon squeezer, the bread-
board. and now the light. they turn and snuggle. counterturn
and balance. like bareback riders in the circus jumping on the
horse's broad back. arms spread. knees slightly bent. relaxed.

yet it's harder than it looks to ride horses or to fall into bed
blending body to body. butt. knees. arms. head have to move
where the gap is. where what rises and what falls fit.

as warmth and drowse overcome them they shift and murmur
less and less. finally. asleep. they separate. here. there. on
and on they go. bareback riders nuzzling the dark. circling on
the dream's broad back till morning wakes them.

then. as day flushes and consciousness spreads. they cling
briefly. but it's too late. turn or counterturn each joins his/her
own body. soon. they will throw off the covers and dismount.
to no one's applause.

it occurred to me the other night, sitting on the john and star-
ing blankly at a bath towel my mouth open, that there's an
awful lot of animal nature in us. my ancestors, Scottish
sheep-herders, probably stared at the hill mist while guarding
sheep, their lives oozing away in front of their noses, nothing
going on but so easy and lovely it was that all was forgiven,
forgotten like the airy mist around them that gathered or
dispersed so intimately, so grandly. and if the sheep died or
gave birth or if their own misfortunes and joys were recorded
it went along with the same animal stare out of a face un-
touched by time and traveling light. no matter the agonies in-
herent in our lives, the bathroom stare redeems us and makes
us one: all things breathing in this same light at the same
level of eternal dumbness which is our gift from the gods.

The Birds and I

it's such a pure waking up
on a summer day for them.
there they are banging away
sparrows chirping close by
like little domestic hens
and in the distance, cardinals
with their clarion call
while all sorts of fluting, warbles
and trills fill the middle air

whereas I open my eyes my hands fisted
sighing in the pearly light
oh dear   oh, dear   oh, dear

I envy such ordinary
and sensible creation
going on and on. every day
surprise! here we are! oh, joy!
the birds are most liquid and exuberant
before the sun comes up
and hunger makes them practical

they wake singing
they don't sigh
don't burn with love
inconsolably
wishing that time would lapse
and they could fall to oblivion

they just do
it's pure surprise and new
every day
for them.

5/3/80

a fine, drizzly rain
I open my face
to the horned moon
on my nightly walk
and revive like a flower
hit with pellets of dew.
dark trees line the road
spiky towering pines
with small ghostly shad
delicate among them.
my dog ranges ahead
checks back when I call
brushing her nose against
my palm — soft as the night
itself. everything soft
breathing easy again.

5/14/80

the first crickets already
sound harsh on the ear
and faintly glowing in the grass
phosphorescent firefly grubs
at night not quite ready
to climb stems and swarm
and a bull-frog at the pond
chunk-chunks in bass vibrato
he's dominant, muddy and deep
and the peepers! I'd forgotten them
they started so far back —
treble with a touch of frost in it
last night a june-bug kept banging my window
attracted by the false light.

9/15/80

the grapes have the bloom on them
they hang in perfect clusters on the vine.
I pick and taste browsing the rows
their globed sweetness tart and cleansing.
later, walking back, my basket full
my shoes are wet with dew.
mist is rising as I descend the hill
and two noisy crows fly overhead.
how nice to move with easy gravity
like a bubble on water riding downstream.

9/18/80

heavy mist this morning in the garden
the wind sounds like sheets of rain
there are birds I can't see out there
twittering in the plum tree
and a phoebe on a wire darts away
it will fly south soon with the others
leaving the woods and the fields empty
the golden promise of summer fulfilled.
only crickets and cicadas will stay
their music grinding the year to bits.

Autumn

a door within the third door opens
a stump appears
covered with moss and mouse turds
dark leaves rustle overhead
and birds spray out in front of us

on the trunk of a tree a wasp
its magenta legs wobbling   stops
it keeps falling asleep then waking up
as a smoky chill descends

at the pond the ducks fly in
I hear them break the surface
the whole weight of the year
pulling them in.

There's a Song in His Throat, Buried

the teenager who wanders the park
at dusk with his portable radio
clamped to his ear is deaf
he told me when I startled him one night
near the deserted beach house

it was eerie and lonely
the waves chopping the shore
the empty life-guard stands
the pods of overturned boats
and, of course the lake
in front of us picking up light that ran
in streaks from houses on the opposite bluffs
like falling tears across the water
the light honed in on us
the heavens were dark, there was wind
and a foretaste of rain

he found it difficult to speak
we had nothing to say
but there's a song buried in his throat
I thought, anyone who'd prowl the beach
at night this way
no friends, nothing to do, hugging loneliness
clamped to his ear and deaf—
now that is a wide expanse to cross
for all of us in there   out here
wandering with no source of light.

The Lover

the world is not lacking in imagination.
there's a mate for nearly everyone
no matter how outrageous the demand.
let a person but touch the door-knob
with sweating palms and window shades
go up all over town. let someone whisper
to their pillow at night. the next day
they'll be singing in the opera.
there's no lack of love.
nothing that can't be done.
a female moth with a molecule of scent
attracts 10,000 males who fly
for miles to reach her side.
all this is true. I've read it.
the most dippy jerk swaggers with love.
I've seen him at the laundromat.
so why can't I reach you
across from me at the table
our hands only inches apart?

This Life

when I left Toronto
in the backseat of Don's car
you appeared running alongside
naked, long red hair streaming
you kept abreast or raced ahead
larger than life leaping
buildings, in clearings
at every click of every pole
the whole landscape absorbed
your pearly skin
till I became dizzy seeing you
here and here and here
this lonely high I was on
fading from Toronto
in the backseat of the car
watching you go by
holding you inside
like a hot stone I'd swallowed.

The Harvest

1. Family

the high bed like a throne and every night
she reads in it then calls him up to bed.

I lay staring intently into the dark.
click of light, whispers. her muffled cries.

my fisted heart speeds threatening to burst.
sex was a dirty, loathsome thing.

parents like animals smeared themselves in it.
left me homeless under the winking stars.

2. *After Dinner*

Dad falls asleep on the couch
a mystery novel open on his heart.
one hand holds it there
the other loosely drags the floor.
he's a heavy harvest.
my sister locks her door;
amid her pubic sweat
she sings to her caged bird, softly.
Mother is polishing silver in the kitchen.
her eyes shine at her
from the buffed sides like full moons
over stagnant water.
in my room I crank the phonograph.
"Anchors Away" fills my ears
with wild sea-dash and spray.
"I could climb...I could climb out of here"
is the old, old refrain
that rises from the house
and settles in the dust of the yard.

3. *To My Sister, Ann*

you told one lover that he bored you
another almost led you to the altar
but he was looking for his mother
and you got away in time.

you finally married the man across the hall
both of you alone on Saturday nights
when cooking smells and family squabbles rose
from below the stairs. it sealed your fate.

thirty years later it's anybody's guess
how you gauge your life
so full of unending middle-class complaints.

I still chafe at mine like a boy
mad at the world. forgive me,
Ann, for sneering at yours so long.
I live alone; keep a dog for company.

4. *April's Child*

my mother is April's child.
she loves flowers and ferny woods.
apple blossoms once sprinkled in her braids.
at eighty she has flower calendars on the wall
and little pots of green everywhere,
her rooms neatly dusted and arranged.
the Texas sun that comes into her kitchen
is the same round, Dutch sun
that cheered her ancestors with its starch
and its order—"life should not be strange."

she holds that admonition firmly;
has no patience with the dark;
she prefers a light social grace.
yet chill and sorrow are always knocking.
friends go down before her eyes.
my father in the hospital a week
and she wouldn't visit him
was angry he was deserting her.
he puzzled, loving, complained,
"where's Mother? where is she?"
there were no funeral rites.
smooth as a turned furrow he left her life.

she has her party days, her bridge cronies,
her arthritis, her pains.
keeps it all brightly going
the shadow at her back, hesitant.
she is April's child and the cooing doves
in the tree outside her window
remind her of home, her father
dropping new pennies in the path
so she would find them. he said,
"it's faery gold." eyes gleaming, breathless
she'd stoop and find in this enchanted world.

5. *Finally*

when I was born God was tired.
Mother sweated and groaned; the forceps pulled;
Father was a true ox of fatherhood.

I was caught in the claws of July.
no time for words, just work to get done.
no red carpets and no rejoicing songs.

I either cried or was too stunned to cry
bounced around as I was after the kingdom
coming to a mundane, subliminal world.

and God, too tired to lift a finger,
raised his eyes and sighed at my birth
saying, "the little that I give, I get."

now I pay as I go pulling words
from His resourceful, remorseless pit
driven neither by pleasure nor pain

but by a convulsive afterbirth of rage
that dares me make something that will last
that will bridge over all that crashes in change.

Silence

I enter it gradually like entering clear water
till it fills me. then I lay back, spread my arms
to greet it and push off. I am floating.
if only I trusted silence completely,
let it carry me all the way to the other shore.
a child on the breast looking up at its mother
that's the kind of silence I mean.

2

The Man and the Young Gardener

Why are tears salty and hot? I'll tell you. Once upon a time in a land of pleasure, honey and gall there lived a man who was growing old. He didn't like it, of course, but he didn't know what to do. His sons were grown and had left home and his wife was no help since she had decided that her magic tortoise was broken and that her only recourse was to grow old and to die a good death.

The man saw no point to this. Nor to her constant discussions of how they should retrench, sell their big house, buy a small one, live near town, accept, accept, finally, the coffin in the ground. Let her wither up and die, he thought. He was not ready. He had an urge to dye his white hair to a pleasant shade of brown − the way it used to be in his youth. But how could he suddenly appear before his friends and acquaintances? They would ask questions or, worse, not say anything but give him snickering or pitying looks. And wouldn't his hair grow out? And, when it rained, wouldn't the dye run?

He thought, next, of keeping himself busy by going to meetings, attending concerts, plays and lectures on up-to-date topics. He also bought a puppy and a kitten to liven up his house. But these activities didn't solve anything because when he came home late at night after a lecture or a play and sat on the edge of his bed to remove his shoes, his bones grumbled and his mind collapsed just like a deflated balloon. And when he looked in the bathroom mirror at the lines in his face and neck, at his lackluster eyes and at his soft paunch, he wondered where his life had gone.

Things went on this dreary way until one day as he was sitting in his study as he usually did in the morning after breakfast, he looked up from his desk which faced a picture window and saw a young man pushing a wheelbarrow in the garden. It was the new gardener! He was tall, thin, loosely gaited and quite handsome − with dark, glossy hair, sporting a neat moustache.

As the man sat there the young man saw him watching and saluted with a friendly but restrained gesture. The man was pleased. And from that day on he made it a habit to greet the gardener from his study window. In fact, he found himself anticipating their silent greeting so much that one day when the gardener didn't show up, the man felt disappointed. He thought of the young man's face, his features, his walk, his patient filling of the wheelbarrow and his slow gait as he wheeled it away. He sighed deeply because the young man was not there and he pined all that day and the next till on the third day — there was the young man again as cheerful and good-looking as if he hadn't been away at all.

The man was so suddenly joyful that he realized he had filled his mind with the young man to the point where the rest of his life was meaningless. What good was anything without the young man's presence? To see his youthful form, his slim hips, his bobbing walk, his shy vigor! The man felt love flood his heart. He didn't account it strange because it was so vivid, so destined. Of course, while he felt all these things he also knew, somewhere, that he was "being a fool." But it made no difference. He was reckless who had been timid all his life.

But shall I go on with the details of how the man came out of his study one day; how he worked alongside the young man and talked to him, finding out about his life; how he tried to woo the young man who was flattered and repelled; how the man suffered being so close and so far away at the same time; how the man turned on the spit of love, roasting in his lust? And how, finally, the young man in his kindness and cruelty told the man that he was too old and awkward to help him in the garden.

Then the man cried hot, salty tears — tears hot as his passion and salty because salt preserves while it kills like the impossible, high waves of the sea trying to overwhelm the land, rising up, then subsiding only to rise again. The man cried for many days in his study pacing back and forth, looking mournfully out the window. Then one day he stopped pacing, dried his eyes, sharpened a pencil, opened a notebook, and sat down at his desk where, without once glancing up, he began to write.

The Last Romantic

1.

the man I love lives among water and trees.
they keep his name cool with their whispering
during the hot summer nights.
then the creek rushes to the lake below
while he sits on a bench outside his door
talking to friends in the evening
and playing his guitar by the light of a lantern
set on flat stones. his voice is low
and level and the massive trees
that surround his house
with lighter patches of night sky above them
loom up to become the limits of the world.
here everything is strangely comforting
for his hands have touched everything –
a kind of miniature paradise he has nourished
but with what continuing pain and regret
I don't think he'll ever say or I'll ever know.

2. Full Moon, July 1978

The moon in July poured through me, caught and saturated the convex earth so thoroughly its beams, from excess, bounced back only to meet new light pouring in.

The shine was a taste on the tongue, a thrill on the body so that I didn't know where to turn — I couldn't avoid it, could only walk and bathe in it or else, partially hidden under a tree, its leaves absorbing some light, peer out bewildered by the moon-face above. It had no shame.

I was looking for him; the love that wasn't returned. Where was he? What would I say to him if he walked toward me in this moony liquid more mysterious than water?

What would he look like in this unreal, transfiguring light? We might be ghosts breathing in unison holding out silvery hands and bodies to one another. We might pass through each other sighing like wind in the trees and rise toward the moon caught in its orbit — to circle it forever drifting in space our pale moon-bellies exposed, genitals open, revolving and revolving, never to touch . . .

I sank down. Now I knew the power of the moon and there was nothing I could do.

3.

I guess love is going outside
yourself in a quiet blaze
toward the other

its sudden birth a shock

how shy you are
how surprised to find yourself
alone out there

the ghost of which body?

will you return?
and, if you do,
can you bear love's answer?

4. *The Invitation*

Come on in, old Lunar Face,
he's not here
you can explore the whole room in
        your cool manner
That's me on the bed
The tiny buckets behind my eyes
        gone dry
you won't see your reflection
        there
and in your gliding you certainly
        won't find him—
the one I waited for all evening.

5. *Refusing to Say Love's Dead*

I wake up in the middle of the night
to a silence that hums your absence
so alive it's a presence in the room.
I say your name to the air
only my breath and a resonance stirs.
I know you're standing by the bed
         I reach my hand out
with slight exaggeration and strain
I can feel you there.

6.

when I talk to him, I keep spitting flowers. they strike him
and immediately melt like huge snowflakes. hitting his eyes
they turn into fringed poppies but are gone in a blink. they hit
his mouth, his chest, his thighs. as they expire they make tiny
sighs like honey-bees so burdened with pollen they can't lift
themselves from the flower. of course, he acts loutish while
this is happening. he grimaces as if to say "look what I have
to put up with!" he goes blank. he yawns. and the snow-
flowers come thick and fast. they are so many, finally, they
stick all over him. little drifts in the folds of his elbows. more
in his lap. it piles up on his shoulders. covers his head like a
cap. clogs his mouth – he never says much to me anyway. his
gestures freeze. his body becomes an outline. and, at last, his
eyes – our one point of contact that tells me he is bruised by
my love as I am bruised – his eyes dim and go. oh, come
back. I promise to stop talking. I'll go away. only come back.
covered in flowers. look at me. say it with your sullen eyes.

7.

that burning, brilliant star
on the western horizon is Mars.
it gleams fiercely just above
the rim of earth
dominates the sky
and has the color of blood.

I drive on a country road
in zero weather, snow covering
everything: barns, fields, woodlots.
I burn in the dark
interior, the star hanging
out the window.

I get the crazy idea
it's you up there, that wild
gleam in your eye, your lean body
become ascendant star
keeping me company.

absurd! yet there you are
as close as my elbow.
my chest tightens.
I fill with cloudy weeping.

8. *You almost loved me.*
                    —V.A.

a cricket and cicada night.
the stars loom through space
and the faint arc of one
falls centuries away—
its story will never reach us.
even so, I leave the doors open.
the rooms line up like empty matchboxes.

*   *   *

the cool circulation of air inside your shirt
after a hot day's work.
I would have sworn to anything pleasurable
knocked my head on the pavement
jumped into the gorge
just to be there
waiting when you walked in.

*   *   *

on its smooth surface
the lake reflects the sky.
cloudy water-lilies open
floating in three worlds.
they know the waves.
they bow before them
as if they were friends.

From the Diary of Peter Doyle

AUTHOR'S NOTE: *Peter Doyle, an ex-Confederate soldier, was 17 when he first met Walt Whitman. They were close friends and frequent companions for six years.*

*   *   *

it was a cold, stormy night. I was working
my horse-car, on late duty, no passengers
when along came this burly, bearded man
blown in by the storm
a blanket thrown over his shoulders.
he got on and sat down, silent.
I looked at him sitting slightly hunched
against the cold – he seemed vigorous
like an old sea-captain.
it was lonely on a lonely night
so I decided to talk to him. something in me
was drawn to him. he was drawn the same way, too.
we were familiar at once. I put my hand on his knee.
we understood. he didn't get out at the end of the trip
in fact went all the way back with me.
from that time on we were the biggest sort of friends.

                    *   *   *

we strolled after work, Walt and I
flowing with the crowds and bustle
Walt waving and talking to everyone
an attraction so genial and open
his eyes warm under his crushed hat with his
long hair and flowing beard like old Father Jove
himself come to walk the world.
he bought me presents:
sweet-meats, candy, a mother-of-pearl knife
with 3 blades. it was great
of an evening to shake loose and drift
the streets with Walt.

                    *   *   *

he's good to me so why do I despair?
worked till 2 a.m. and there was Walt
waiting. we went on a moonlight ramble
through the Capitol, past the White House
down the long avenues the streets deserted
finally resting on the bank of the Potomac
the water shivered with thousands of silver fish
Walt started to explain the constellations
his voice so deep and tender I fell asleep
woke, startled, to his calm grey eyes
in the morning light, his coat over me
said he got used to sitting up all night
with wounded soldiers. his face looked
the way an angel's face might, stepping on thorns:
full of love and pain and so far away
I was jealous. but *I* ain't wounded, I said
I got the use of *all* my limbs and faculties
meaning a joke. he got up kinda hurried
called me "son." embraced me. I went home to bed.

*   *   *

I am ugly I know
my complexion is like sour milk
it turns their stomachs —
girls, I mean, from the most dainty
to the gross ones who slop beer
on my pants at table

but you, Walt, you look through
my craters on the moon
with such soft puzzlement
like I held a key you couldn't turn
in a dream and it means a lot
or like I was the head-waters of the Nile
and you the first man to find them!
what do you want of me?
I feel like I'm some kind of cosmic joke.

*   *   *

when I got home tonight
there was a bouquet of flowers:
a bunch of hairy-tongued iris
small pink roses, some daffodil.
struck me blank at first
but it was Walt, all right.

*   *   *

I'm so low down blue and miserable
my face all broken out with barber's itch
I feel so bad I could throw myself under a train
get sliced up but damned pieces would just
continue throbbing with more pain
more misery, spread around more
like smashing a wasp's nest with a stick.

*   *   *

it's almost like a marriage
and that *almost* is what kills...

*　　*　　*

he took me to the Doctor to see about my face
he has clothes made for me – rough flannel
shirts, the kind he wears himself
he lends me money when I need it
gives me good advice about my job
wants me to advance and get along
sends me bouquets of flowers
embraces me, kisses me, is doting
and loving. calls me "son," "brother," "dear boy,"
"darling," "baby," calls himself "your old man"
so why do I despair get blue and low-down
threaten to kill myself so he's upset
and angry?...

I could tell you why, Walt,
but I can't. you're the good grey poet,
so pure and manly he never sins and though
the world calls your writing obscene and dirty
your followers, some very important men,
know different. I guess I know, too,
your kisses so hearty and so neutral!

*   *   *

I've read "Leaves of Grass," the Calamus poems.
in fact I have my own Calamus songs, Walt.
they're not like yours innocent and ideal
though it comes to the same thing:
the damn writing is just make-believe
and everything close and real about us sinks out of sight.

*   *   *

at least I know there's something more to us
while you fuss and evade like a mother hen.
I love you, Walt, and understand your need
for fame. I was willing. oh, so willing
to give and that's what hurts. the body
insists on having its way—
not to break and unravel slowly to the end.

*   *   *

after your stroke and my taking care of you
you said you'd mend and it'd be old times
but I knew, Walt, it was a plea for me
to pretend. so, I'll pretend whatever you say
and I'll write you a letter once a week
but I won't come visit you in Camden.

*   *   *

I was turned away at your funeral
till someone recognized me and led me in.
I saw you, Walt, stretched out
serene and olympian—a bit waxy and
rouge-flushed, but you'd made it.
one of their immortals at last.

I didn't break down—not there anyway.
the crowds, your gentleman friends
fussing, the newsmen—made our being
together unreal. not till I got home
and remembered the night I fell asleep
on your shoulder—the warmth and shagginess
of your grey shawl on my cheek
your solid chest beneath like a cavern
near the sea full of mysterious sighs
and quiverings, a universe that grew
forever so it seemed—did I cry
for us, Walt, blind and exhausted.

*   *   *

200 dollars and a gold watch in your will
for me, Walt! I never saw either the money
or the watch—hear you gave them to another
boy instead.

*   *   *

for those eight years of love and suffering
spent with my youth in tow, I say
goodbye, you have them. I move easy among
railroad men and do my job
do what I can each day, remember
the good times — they're mine
exclusive. I wake to them
every morning, Walt, like a soft fog
that rolls in overnight and leaves its taste
metallic and burning on my tongue.

Calamus Songs of Peter Doyle

Walt, Walt, Walt,
may you dream something good about me
may a seed be planted
that will grow up around your heart
spread to the tip of your nose
then to your ears to hear love growing
to your eyes to count 1, 2, 3, and to see
to your mouth, your baby teeth grinning
to your tongue to tell it, to your chin
that ledge on the world greeting me
and down your arms to your fingertips
those strong currents and moons of energy
then to your chest like a diver to echo it,
across your paddled stomach to pause and listen
to the omphalos, the center of the world
then down the soft hair of your thighs
past your toes that grip, silly and singular
and then back up and out, out to
(what can I say more?) your sweet pecker, Walt,
where my love will finally flower.

                    *   *   *

I'm the slight, stringy type
with soulful eyes
and a moustache that bites
I look a bit of a rat
but my kisses
and tongue-dancing
its pressures and suction
its tight gothic curl
its fine soupy gliding
would keep you buzzing
keep you flopping
half the night
dear, passive Walt.

                    *   *   *

I'm languid
I'm liquid
I'm ready
enter me, Walt,
the way velvet curtains
part at the opera
a miniature world
suspended, hushed,
waiting
for the full-throated tenor
the heavier bass
to roar
I'll be the love-struck
heroine
I'll sing soprano
hit the high notes
right off the scale.

now that I'm in Heaven, Walt,
and I *mean* Heaven.
where the days run on forever
and love is centuries long
I am a boy again
thoughtless and happy

yet back there
in the nether darkness
I left a seed of light.
Walt, guard it for me.

Stations of Love

I think I'll live in a windy cave away from people. away from
you at least. with bottle flies. mosquitoes. whistling bats at
night. the lesser, humble creation to minister to me to cure
me of this burning in my marrow when I leave you. I can't
even phrase your body. the light in your eyes. the whole appe-
tite of sensation. but I burn and get cold and am eaten like a
wolf at my belly just thinking about you − waking up with a
start to stare at the wall. away! away! there is no one like you.
oh my God. what have I done? what is happening to me?

*   *   *

just a trickle of water wearing the stone that's how it started:
you. you. you. until I saw that the lines in my body had changed
caressed continually by your weight − not physically. but
worse. the shadow substance of your spirit throwing its light
my way so freely. so casually I cried out in pain.

*   *   *

can I learn to live with the despair of loving you? the man was
hit on the head with the butt end of a pistol. he woke up. was
hit again. what am I saying! you swim before my eyes. I am
floating toward a galaxy of grinning faces that recede. no
harm meant it is just a trick of yours I have to absorb.

*   *   *

I fail you at every breath. when I should close in I drift away. you say something. I am deaf. you point and my eyes glaze. how you keep patience I don't know. this sea I swim in feels like land to me. these lights like velvet darkness. my left. my right. nebulous. I whinny and whine. all my tricks are evasions of you.

*   *   *

I love you. somewhere in your heart you'll have to forgive my awkwardness. my fragile hesitations. you who pronounce yourself so wisely your hands spread on the table. I smile at your words the way children do at anything. it's time to be giddy and reverent. there are worse things than being a fool.

*   *   *

can I put love in my heart? stuff it there? I feel nothing most of the time. anesthetized by walking up and down. though I register the kindness. the folly. the self centered on its pin and whirling. there is always the desperate wind. I know that. so it is pity I feel. but love! who can speak of its hush. its pause before stepping out. it is so shy. "always in danger."

*   *   *

maybe we'll leave each other alone now. that's a possibility. a calm lake between us. nothing to shatter. but that is my lying fantasy. up from the depths. damn-it! the water-snake on the surface. the buffalo throwing spray. snorting its freedom. its disbelief. the stars refracted in its wake. swaying points of light. ports of call. and home somewhere out there dawn gathers.

*   *   *

I'll rise up shining and bathe everyone in light. now I know why angels lord it over creation. blow trumpets in the four quarters. marshal spirits. they are bold with matter. making it weightless heaven. everyone's dream of feathers and flame. an embracing desert of hunger. a pit of longing. a sky so blank that dead eyes reflect it totally. on that new day.

About the Author

John Gill lives near Taughannock Falls, on a ridge above Cayuga Lake, near Ithaca, New York. He and his wife Elaine were pioneers in the small press movement. They began by publishing *NEW: American and Canadian Poetry*, a highly regarded little magazine of the 1960s, and after leaving academe made The Crossing Press their livelihood. Gill's years of editing the poetry magazine culminated in *New American and Canadian Poetry*, an important anthology which he edited for the Beacon Press in 1971. Readers of this book may wish to obtain the only other collection of his poetry still in print, *Country Pleasures*, published in 1975 by The Crossing Press, Trumansburg, New York 14886.